Working Animals

by Anne Giu

a Capstone company — publishers for children

Engage Literacy is published in the UK by Raintree.
Raintree is an imprint of Capstone Global Library Limited, a company incorporated in England and Wales
having its registered office at 264 Banbury Road, Oxford, OX2 7DY – Registered company number: 6695582

www.raintree.co.uk

Editorial credits
Erika L. Shores, editor; Richard Parker, designer; Pam Mitsakos, media researcher;
Katy LaVigne, production specialist

Image credits
Alamy: dpa picture alliance, 16, epa european pressphoto agency b.v., 19; Getty Images: Steve Bly, 13; iStockphoto:
Davor Lovincic, 11, gjohnstonphoto, 14 bottom right, kuban_girl, 18; Science Source, Disability Images, 23;
Shutterstock: 1000 Words, 6 bottom right, anetapics, back cover, Cylonphoto, 6 bottom left, Daz Stock, 5 middle
right, deepspace, 20-21, f9photos, cover middle right, gillmar, 1, 9, john michael evan potter, 5 top left, Katiekk, 22,
kikujungboy, 7, Marianna Kalashnyk, design element, Michaelpuche, 8, Mikkel Bigandt, 12, Monika Wisniewska, 15,
Perry Correll, cover middle left, pirita, 4, Ricardo Canino, 5 bottom left, salajean, 10, Sergey Krasnoshchokov, cover
bottom; SuperStock: FLPA, 14 bottom middle; Thinkstock: Huntstock, 17
Glossary:
Shutterstock: _plaza_, (alarm), Aghidel, (falcon), bigredlynx, (coyotes), GraphicsRF, (desert), hugotunes, (huskies),
Ingaga, (cart), Lorelyn Medina, (herding), Macrovector, (guard), MuchMania, (transportation), Skalapendra, (carriage),
Sky vectors, (forests), Svitlana Belinska, (draft), Tarikdiz, (loads)

10 9 8 7 6 5 4 3 2 1
Printed and bound in China.

Working Animals

ISBN: 978 1 4747 3908 5

Contents

Animals everywhere

There are many different animals
in the world.
Some are large, and others are small.
Animals can move in many ways
and live almost anywhere.
All animals are special in their own way.

horse

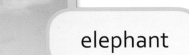
elephant

dog

dolphin

On the job

Animals can be kept as pets,
but they can also work.
When animals work they need
to be trained by people.
It can take months and sometimes
even years to train them to do a job.

Animals that do special jobs
are called working animals.
There are many different jobs
they can do to help people.
Working animals can move and carry.
They can push, pull and find things or people.
Some of them can even work in films!

Animals used for transport

Animals can be used to move or *transport* people.

Horses can move people from one place to another.

A person can ride a horse or a horse can be used to pull a *carriage* or *cart*.

In very cold places where there is a lot of snow, dogs called *huskies* pull people on sledges.

donkeys

Draught animals

Donkeys, camels and elephants
work as *draught* animals.
A draught animal moves heavy things or *loads*.
The animals need to be very strong.
They have to work in places
such as the *desert*, jungle or mountains.

camels

Herding animals

Moving animals in a group from one place to another is called *herding*.

Many farmers use dogs to herd their sheep, cattle and even ducks!

Dogs that herd work to keep all of the animals together.

Guard animals

Animals can also be used to watch over or *guard* something.
They help keep other animals safe.

Animals such as alpacas and llamas can be used to watch over sheep, goats and even chickens.
Alpacas and llamas make noise when the other animals are in danger. They can also kick or chase foxes or *coyotes* away.
The guard animals can herd the sheep, goats and chickens to a safe place.

llama

sheep with alpaca

Dogs can also be used to guard things.
A dog's loud bark keeps buildings
or cars safe.

Some dogs are trained to use their noses
to smell things.
Then they can let people know
if there is danger.

Helping people

Animals can be trained to help people who can't see or hear.

People who can't see often use special dogs to see for them.

These dogs help people who are blind to do everyday things, such as shopping and crossing the road.

People who can't hear also use dogs
to help them.
These dogs can let people know if someone
is at the door.
They can also let them know if an *alarm*
has gone off and even if a baby is crying.

Animal stars

Dogs, cats and birds are used
in films and on TV.
So are dolphins and horses.
They are trained to do special things.
They can make people feel sad
or make people laugh.
Some film star animals can even do
special tricks.

Search and rescue animals

Dogs can be trained to use their noses to sniff out and find people who are lost. These dogs are called search and rescue dogs.
Sometimes these dogs have to look in *forests*, deserts or broken buildings to find people that need help.

Animals used for hunting

Some animals are used for hunting, too.
In deserts where it is hard to find food,
a bird called a *falcon* can be trained
to help people hunt.

Working animals are trained
to help in many ways.
They help to move things
and keep people safe.
They are used
to find things and
people and hunt, too.
What other working
animals can you
think of?
What other ways can
they help us?

Picture glossary

alarm

draught

huskies

carriage

falcon

loads

cart

forests

transport

coyotes

guard

desert

herding